A Crown for Christ

An Imaginative Lent to Easter Programme for Children

Family • School • Church

Katie Thompson

GW00586447

kevin mayhew

First published in 2002 by
KEVIN MAYHEW LTD
Buxhall, Stowmarket, Suffolk IP14 3BW
E-mail info@kevinmayhewltd.com

9 8 7 6 5 4 3 2 1 0

ISBN 1 84003 991 4
Catalogue No 1500552

Cover design by Jonathan Stroulger
Edited by James Croft
Typesetting by Richard Weaver

Printed in Great Britain

Contents

Introduction								5

A crown for Christ							7

The jewel of service							10

The jewel of courage							13

The jewel of peace							15

The jewel of truthfulness						18

The jewel of acceptance						21

The jewel of strength (fortitude)					23

The jewel of humility							25

The jewel of compassion (being kind-hearted)			27

The jewel of forgiveness						29

The jewel of hope							33

The jewel of thoughtfulness						35

The jewel of love							40

The jewel of joy							44

Recipes								47

Templates								48

Introduction

Jesus said, 'My kingdom is not a worldly kingdom, or my armies would have fought to save me. But that is not my kind of kingdom.' 'But you are indeed a king?' asked Pilate the Roman Governor. 'Yes,' Jesus replied, 'I am a king who was born into the world for this; to be a witness to the truth, and all who are truthful listen to my voice.'

John 18:36-38

Jesus is like no other king the world has ever known. As a man he had no earthly palace, no worldly treasure, and his only crown was made of thorny twigs. To him, jewels and riches aren't precious stones such as diamonds or emeralds, but virtues and qualities such as courage, faith, love and forgiveness. Jesus is our perfect example of goodness and virtue. By sharing these jewels with the world, he shows us how our words and actions can help us to follow him to his loving kingdom.

Before we celebrate Easter, we recall the final journey he made upon his way to the cross, and learn more about what kind of king Jesus really is. Each jewel along the way highlights what qualities make a person truly rich in the eyes of God, and reminds us that our goodness is more precious than any treasure could ever be.

Christ's only crown was made of thorny twigs cruelly pressed into his noble and gentle head. Yet he deserved a crown adorned with the most precious stones and beautiful jewels, a crown fit to be worn by the Prince of Peace and King of Glory. This book will help you to create such a crown for Christ. Instead of diamonds, rubies and sapphires, it will be decorated with 'jewels' that are more cherished than any rare or precious stone. Your loving effort and time will make a crown more valuable to Jesus than any earthly treasure could ever be.

This practical resource for young people is intended to help them to prepare for Easter in a fresh, enjoyable and meaningful way. As they share in the events and feelings experienced by Jesus before his death and resurrection, they focus on the 'jewels' or virtues of goodness revealed by the things he said and did on his way to the cross. Through reflection and prayer, they can learn more about the person of Jesus, and by relating these virtues to the circumstances and experiences of their own young lives, understand how they can personally follow him better.

This material is sufficiently flexible to be used imaginatively with a broad spectrum of age groups, including young people within a parish community, schools searching for a new direction and ideas, families wanting to add meaning to the events of Holy Week and anyone who wants to approach the Easter celebrations from a new perspective with fresh guidance for personal or group reflection.

The suggestions for reflections, prayers and activities should be adapted or used appropriately for the specific needs and capabilities of the individuals or groups using them. The readings and activities can be split between the six Sundays leading up to Easter, or used as a meditation on the Way of the Cross during Holy Week itself. Use the material as a springboard which inspires your imagination and encourages you to develop and use your own creative ideas.

By sharing the final journey of Jesus, it is possible to pause along the way to think about the jewels of faith and love he continued to share with the world right up until the moment of his death. Whether as individuals or within groups, you can create a crown that is worthy for Christ the king of love.

A crown for Christ

Create a cross

Begin by making a large, simple cross from two wooden cross-pieces or branches bound together with rope. Depending on the space available, and the size of your cross, it can either be laid on the floor using a piece of red or purple fabric as a backdrop, or securely anchored in a heavy pot or stand, filled with pebbles or damp sand. The crown (or crowns) you create can then be displayed on or next to this cross.

Following in his footsteps

As we share Christ's final journey to the cross and dress his crown with jewels, young people can focus on their own journey as Christians trying to follow in his footsteps.

Hand- and footprints made with paint (see Recipes, p. 47) can provide a fun way to emphasise uniqueness and individuality, and how each person must find their own particular way to follow Christ.

Footprint 1

You will need . . .

- Paint and brush
- Paper for printing
- Newspaper or old piece of vinyl or carpet
- Bowl of warm water, soap and old towel
- Old tray

Protect the floor with newspaper or a suitable covering. Pour sufficient paint onto the tray to cover it generously when spread with a brush. Lay out paper to print onto. Step onto the paint with bare feet, and then carefully step out onto the paper to make your prints. Step onto some newspaper before carefully washing your feet! (A similar method could be used for handprints.)

Footprint 2

You will need . . .

- Paper
- Pencils or pens
- Scissors

Carefully draw around a left foot and cut out the shape. Now use this shape as a template to copy and cut out. This second shape provides a corresponding opposite foot. (To save time, such shapes could simply be photocopied.) Such footprints can be used in several different ways; for example:

1. Cut out the corresponding number of footprints for each jewel in the crown. These can be made into individual books, which are joined at the

'heel' or along the length of the foot. Do this by stapling or using a hole-punch and threading with string, wool, ribbon or similar. These little books can be used to record thoughts and ideas as the young people listen to, and reflect upon, Christ's journey to the cross. They could draw pictures of each Gospel scene, with a corresponding thought or prayer; they could include a symbol for each jewel and something about what it means to them. The ideas are endless; simply use your imagination.

2. The footprints could be used to form an eye-catching Lenten wall display representing the children's journey towards the cross and the joy of Easter that follows. Starting at a distant point, a copy of the first Gospel story is displayed on coloured background paper cut into the shape of a jewel such as a diamond. Each jewel should be clearly annotated and ideally be accompanied by some explanation about the particular symbol chosen to represent it on the crown you create. The young people's individual footprints with their own prayers, pictures, reflections or stories about each jewel, should be attractively arranged around it. By the time the final jewel is reached, you should have a colourful stream of footprints making their way towards the cross.

Create a crown

Several suggestions are made for 'crown' displays, but don't be afraid to make the ideas in this book fit your own particular circumstances, resources and capabilities. A large crown made from brambles or similar might not be a practical option, so use the idea in an alternative way to satisfy your particular needs. Consider using different materials such as cardboard, wire, papier-mâché or coloured paper or card. If a floor display is not feasible, then consider adapting it to create a wall display, place it on a stand or hang it as a mobile. Adapt the symbol suggestions to make them suitable for your crown, whether it is freestanding, hanging or displayed on the wall. Hopefully the suggestions made will help to ignite your imagination and enthusiasm, and stimulate and encourage your own creative and original ideas.

Crown 1

For authenticity, thorny branches or brambles should ideally be used to make this crown, but for practical reasons of safety, lengths of ivy carefully stripped of leaves or thornless branches or twigs are perfectly adequate alternatives. Collect several branches and carefully overlap them before tying them together with string or raffia. Fill a bucket or similar container with warm water and carefully lower the branches in. As they soften in the water, slowly bend them around the inside of the bucket to form a circle. Tie the branches in several places to hold the circle firmly in position. Leave the crown to soak for approximately 24 hours before emptying the bucket. Leave the branches inside the bucket until they are completely dry and retain their shape. The string can then be carefully removed. The size of the crown you choose to make can obviously be scaled up or down depending on the length of branches or twigs you use and the circumference of the container in which they are soaked and subsequently dried. The crown can now be adorned with the appropriate symbolic 'jewels'.

Crown 2

Cut out one large crown from metallic or coloured card (or similar) using the template on page 48, or enough crowns to provide one each. These can then be decorated in a variety of ways depending on the type of materials you wish to use, and the time and resources that are available. Several suggestions are given, but with imagination and resourcefulness a great deal of enjoyment and fun can be gained from designing your own original ways of producing decorative details. The decoration of each crown can be as simple or complicated as you choose to make it. Ideally each jewel should be represented by either a different shape, colour or type of material depending on which method you choose to use. This makes it easier to relate each jewel on the crown to the virtue it represents.

Some suggestions for decorative details:

- Carefully cut out 13 diamond 'windows' from the crown. Different colours of tissue paper or cellophane can then be glued or taped inside the crown to cover each diamond-shaped 'window'. These represent the 'jewels' as they are added one by one.

- Use gummed or self-adhesive paper shapes available from most good newsagents or art shops.

- Cut your own designs and shapes from sheets of foil or metallic/decorative paper or card.

- Use old buttons and brighten them up with glitter, nail polish or poster paints.

- Milk bottle tops and coloured foil sweet wrappers.

- Paper snowflake shapes cut from thin card or coloured paper. (Cut a circle of card or paper and fold in half three times. Snip small pieces from the sides and open out to reveal your design.)

- Different shapes of dried pasta shells or pulses. (These can be painted, or decorated with nail polish or glitter.)

- Pieces of braid or ribbon, sequins, beads, lace, and decorative string, thread or cord could all be used.

- All sorts of paper in different colours and textures.

The jewel of service

Jesus washes his disciples' feet

It was just before the Passover celebration, and knowing that the time for him to die was fast approaching, Jesus showed his disciples the depth of his love for them.

While they were at supper together, Jesus stood up and, laying his outer garments to one side, he wrapped a towel around his waist. The disciples watched as he fetched a basin of water and knelt down to wash their feet one by one, before drying them with the towel.

When it was Peter's turn, he protested loudly, 'Lord, it isn't right that you should wash my feet!'

But gently Jesus insisted, and reluctantly Peter allowed his master to wash his feet.

When he had finished, Jesus dressed and returned to the table. 'Just as your Lord and Master has washed your feet, so you must be ready to do for others what I have done for you.'

Then he told them, 'This is my new commandment: love one another as I have loved you. The world will know that you are my disciples by the love you have for one another.'

Adapted from John 13:1-15, 34-35

Reflection

Have you ever washed the feet of another person? It is probably not something most of us would enjoy doing, or indeed having done to us. Feet are often thought of as being rather unattractive parts of our bodies. At the time when Jesus lived, people generally wore sandals, and their feet would have been dusty and dirty. It was the task of a servant or slave to wash the feet of others, but Jesus did not choose to wash his disciples' feet because there was no servant to do so. He took on the role of servant to show his friends in a way that they could clearly understand, how he wanted his followers to serve one another. His actions spoke more clearly than any words. He gave us a remarkable example of how to make our lives like his. He washed their feet as an expression of his deep love for them. The hands which had healed the sick, fed the hungry, made the blind see, and raised the dead to life, gently washed their feet because of that love. The Son of God was ready to serve, and asked his disciples to do the same.

God calls us to serve him and one another in different ways. Our ordinary lives and the ordinary things we do and say, are our daily service of God. Any work or task can be boring or frustrating at times, but if we do it cheerfully with love, even ordinary tasks can become deeply satisfying and enjoyable. We must put our feelings of pride aside and serve one another lovingly and with complete humility. Our loving actions and attitudes towards one another mark us out as disciples of Christ. In every act of love and service offered in every home, school, workplace and hospital, it is his love we give, receive and share with one another in our everyday lives.

Focus

- Why do you think that Peter did not want Jesus to wash his feet?
- How do you imagine the disciples felt to see their Master behaving like a servant?
- Think of the different ways various people have served you recently or today (at home or school, in shops or on journeys). How did you respond to their acts of service?
- In what different ways in our everyday lives can we serve one another?

Service can make a difference – a story for reflection . . .

A person asked God, 'How is heaven different from hell?' 'Come, and I will show you,' God replied. First they visited hell and entered a room where everyone sat around a hot, steaming pot of delicious food. Everyone there was desperately hungry. Each person had a spoon which reached the pot, but whose handle was so long that they could not manoeuvre the spoon laden with food into their own mouths. The smell of the delicious food made their mouths water, and they cried with frustration and pangs of hunger.

Then God took the person to visit heaven. They entered another room which appeared identical in every detail. It had a similar pot of delicious food and people sat gathered around it. As before, each had a long-handled spoon, but unlike before, everyone appeared happy and content, and no one went hungry. 'How can they be so happy when the others were so miserable?' God was asked. God smiled and answered, 'Because in heaven, they feed one another.'

Prayer

Heavenly Father,
it can be difficult to serve others!
Often our own selfish thoughts and needs get in the way.
Sometimes others make it awkward for us to love them as you ask.
Help us to find some way each day
to show the world how much we care.
We make our prayer through Christ our King,
Amen.

Symbols

The symbols of towels and feet remind us of the jewel of service when Christ washed the feet of his disciples.

Towels

You will need . . .

- Coloured paper or pieces of fabric
- Scissors
- Hole-punch
- Gold thread

- Felt-tip pens
- Glue, glitter, sequins (optional)

Cut out small rectangular shapes of paper or fabric. Use scissors to carefully cut fringes along both ends of the rectangle. Colour or decorate the towels brightly. Use a hole-punch to make a hole and loop some gold thread through to attach to the crown.

Feet

You will need . . .

- Paint and an old plate
- Cocktail sticks
- Cotton buds
- Can of kidney beans or old washing-up sponges
- Paper
- Scissors
- Sellotape
- Gold thread

Rinse and drain the kidney beans, and allow to dry. Place two beans side by side, with the concave sides facing each other. Carefully skewer each bean with a cocktail stick (an adult should do this for younger children), and dip them onto a plate of paint, before printing each alternately onto a sheet of plain paper. (This should produce a set of prints.) Dip the end of a cotton bud onto the paint, and carefully make five 'toe' prints above each kidney bean print. Allow to dry before carefully cutting out the matching feet. Sellotape a length of thread to each foot, tie a knot or loop at the top and hang on the crown display. (As an alternative to kidney beans, cut foot-shaped templates from an old washing-up sponge and use as described above.)

The jewel of courage

The agony in the Garden

When they reached the Garden of Gethsemane, Jesus told his disciples to wait for him while he went to pray. Taking Peter, James and John with him, Jesus said to them, 'Keep watch with me and pray my friends, for tonight my heart is heavy', and indeed he was filled with great fear and sorrow at the thought of his approaching death. Jesus moved a little further away, before throwing himself on the ground and praying, 'Father, everything is possible for you. Save me from this suffering, but if it is your will, then I will do whatever you ask.'

When he returned to his friends, Jesus was saddened to find them asleep. 'Could you not stay awake and pray with me?' he asked. 'Keep watch and pray you don't give in to sleep.'

Once more he went off alone to pray, and once more he returned to find his companions fast asleep.

When this happened for a third time, Jesus said to them, 'Now you have slept enough! The time has come for the Son of Man to be betrayed and handed over.'

Adapted from Mark 14:32-42

Reflection

We have all experienced fear at some time in our lives. It is a powerful emotion, which can be extremely unpleasant. Feelings of fear and anxiety make our hearts pound, our stomachs feel sick, and our bodies break out in a sweat. Scientists explain that such bodily responses to fear prepare us to 'take flight' to escape whatever makes us feel threatened and afraid.

As Jesus knelt in the Garden of Gethsemane he was afraid. In the stillness of the dark night, with his heart pounding loudly, he sadly waited for his accusers to come and arrest him. He did not hide his fear, and turned to his heavenly Father praying that there might be another way. However afraid he felt, he did not run away. He accepted what had to happen, and overcame his fear of the suffering and death which awaited him. Jesus undoubtedly had courage, a word that comes from the French word 'coeur' meaning 'heart'.

A courageous person has a big heart which loves deeply, and Jesus was about to show the world the depth of his love by dying on the cross. As Christians, there will be times in our lives when we will need courage and heart to overcome difficulties or times of uncertainty. We might feel afraid and inadequate to cope with the challenges and tests we experience in our ordinary lives. At such times we can draw comfort and reassurance from the knowledge that Jesus understands and shares our fears and will help us to have the courage we need.

Focus

• Do you or someone you know have any particular fears or phobias?

• How do they make you feel and what happens?

- Read Luke 22:41-44. What does this tell you about how Jesus felt?
- Now read Matthew 26:56. How did the disciples react to fear?
- Have you ever needed to have courage?
- How do we overcome feelings of fear and anxiety?
- In what ways do followers of Christ have to be courageous today in their everyday lives?

Prayer

Heavenly Father,
often we find it hard to be brave and courageous.
It is easier to run away,
to be afraid.
As we turn to you,
at times of trouble,
just as Jesus did,
give us the courage
to choose your way,
to accept your will
and to trust in your love.
We make our prayer through Christ our King,
Amen.

Symbols

The symbols of rope and chains are used to represent Christ's courage as he waited to be arrested and led away.

Rope

You will need . . .

- A selection of garden twine, string or thick wool
- Sellotape

Simply cut the twine or material of choice into short lengths. Carefully unravel and fray each end for a short distance, and secure with a knot or by wrapping a thin strip of Sellotape above the frayed end. These lengths of 'rope' can be woven among the branches of the crown.

Chain

You will need . . .

- Small lengths of chain from old necklaces, handbag straps, etc.
- Scissors

Carefully cut the chain into small lengths and add to the crown. (As an alternative, cut thin strips of metallic paper or aluminium foil and use these to make lengths of paper chain.)

The jewel of peace

The arrest of Jesus

A crowd led by Judas appeared in the Garden. As Judas walked up to Jesus and went to kiss him, Jesus asked, 'Will you betray the Son of Man with a kiss?'

When his disciples realised what was happening, they shouted to Jesus, 'Lord, shall we use our swords?' At that moment, one of them struck out and cut an ear off the high priest's servant.

But Jesus stopped them, saying, 'Enough, no more!' And he reached out and healed the man's ear.

Adapted from Luke 22:47-51

Reflection

A crowd armed with clubs and swords came to arrest Jesus under cover of darkness. They were prepared for a violent clash with the followers of Jesus, expecting them to fight to protect and defend the master whom they loved. Indeed as Judas stepped forward to betray Jesus with a kiss, the disciples' anger did momentarily boil over, as one of them struck out and wounded the High Priest's servant. As violence threatened to erupt, Jesus intervened, astounding those who stood ready to defend him, by telling them to lay down their weapons. Then in the midst of so much anger and hatred, he reached out and healed his enemy with a gentle touch. His words and actions restored peace and calm and prevented anyone else from being hurt. He stood as a person of peace shining among the darkness of the people of violence.

It is not easy to be a peacemaker. Often people are unwilling to listen, to forgive, to try to understand or to compromise. Efforts at reconciliation can meet with violent opposition, ridicule or scorn. But Jesus left us in no doubt about what he expects from his followers. As children of God the world should recognise us as people of peace.

Focus

- Does fighting solve arguments?
- In which countries of the world is there conflict and violence today? What efforts are being made to restore peace there?
- What qualities do you think a peacemaker might need?
- Have you ever acted as a peacemaker at home, school or with your friends?

Prayer

Heavenly Father,
may our words and actions
bring peace and harmony,
transforming hatred to love,

despair to hope,
sadness to joy,
and darkness to light.
We make our prayer through Christ our King,
Amen.

Symbol

Traditional symbols of peace include the dove and the olive branch or leaf. Together with a sword, these are used to remind us of the events which occurred when Jesus was arrested in Gethsemane.

Dove

You will need . . .

- Thin white card or paper
- Gold thread
- White bun cases
- Double-sided Sellotape or glue
- Scissors

Cut out a dove shape from paper or card. Take a single bun case and fold it in half, and then in half again. Either open it out and cut along the folds you have made to produce four small 'wings', or use as folded to give a three-dimensional effect. Use a small piece of double-sided Sellotape or glue to attach the wings to your cut out dove. Alternatively, fold a sheet of white paper and complete the dove as illustrated. Hang the dove from the crown with gold thread.

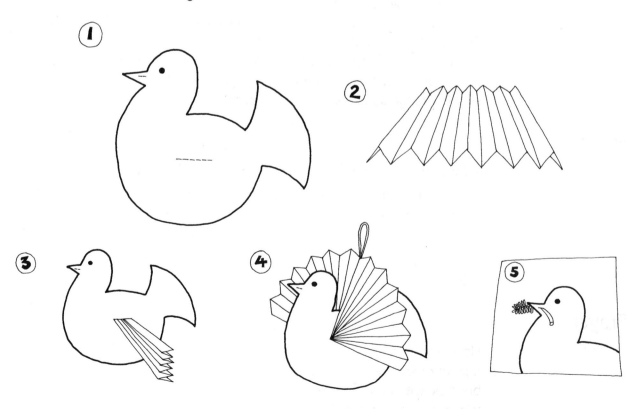

Olive leaves

You will need . . .

- Green paper
- Scissors
- Green florist's wire or pipe cleaners
- Sellotape

Cut leaf shapes from the green paper. Fold each leaf in half lengthways. Use the scissors to make small cuts along the edges (not along the fold!). Tape a short length of wire or similar along the centre of the leaf and use this to attach it to the crown.

(Several leaves and stems could be intertwined to create a branch effect.)

Sword

You will need . . .

- Thin metallic card
- Double-sided Sellotape
- Cocktail sticks
- Corks or polystyrene
- Glue
- Gold thread
- Scissors
- Twine, string or wool

Draw the shape of a sword blade and cut out. Use this template to cut blade shapes from the metallic card. (Each sword will need two shapes, which are glued back to back.) Place one half of a blade with its metallic or shiny side facing downwards. Sellotape a cocktail stick on top, leaving enough protruding to make a handle. Carefully stick the other half of the knife blade on top. Take a circular slice of cork or a piece of polystyrene and carefully push the end of the cocktail stick through. (An adult should do this for younger children.) Next stick a piece of double-sided Sellotape around the handle and then wrap a length of twine, string or wool around this. Secure by tying a length of gold thread firmly around the handle to attach to the crown. (As an alternative to metallic card, simply wrap and stick some aluminium foil around some ordinary card.)

The jewel of truthfulness

Jesus is questioned and condemned

Then Caiaphas the High Priest asked Jesus, 'Tell me, are you indeed the Christ, the Son of God?'

'I am,' Jesus replied. 'And you will see the Son of Man seated on God's right-hand and coming on the clouds of heaven.'

At these words, Caiaphas leapt to his feet and tore his clothes. 'We have no need of witnesses now,' he cried loudly. 'We have heard this evidence with our own ears! This man has insulted God, and the punishment for such blasphemy is death! What is your verdict?'

Then the whole assembly agreed that he deserved to die.

Adapted from Mark 14:61-64

Reflection

Would you tell the truth even if your life depended on it? If we are really honest, most people would take the easy way out and say whatever would get them out of trouble. Jesus had done nothing wrong and his accusers could find no evidence to condemn him. Even the witnesses who lied against him could not convince the court of his guilt. Jesus was sentenced to die because he answered the High Priest's question truthfully. When asked, 'Are you the Son of God?' he replied, 'I am.' Jesus stood up for the truth and what was right, even though he knew that his words gave his enemies the evidence they needed to put him to death.

Every day we have choices to make in our ordinary lives about whether or not to be truthful. Honesty and truth always stand on the side of goodness and what is right. Truthfulness helps us to choose to do what is right even when that choice might be really difficult.

Focus

- Can you think of an occasion when you were dishonest and told a lie? (Sharing is not necessary!)
- How did telling a lie make you feel?
- Has telling the truth ever got you into trouble? What happened?
- If someone tells lies or untruths about you, how does it make you feel?
- Read Mark 14:55-59. How do you imagine Jesus felt?
- How do you think Christians today suffer for speaking the truth about their faith and what they believe?

Prayer

Heavenly Father,
may the Spirit of truth
guide and lead us
so that our words

become your words,
because your word is truth.
We make our prayer through Christ our King,
Amen.

Symbol

The symbols of an execution order and a question mark are used as reminders of Christ's truthful answer to the question asked by Caiaphas the High Priest.

Execution order

You will need . . .

- Sheets of white paper or baking parchment
- Double-sided Sellotape
- Wooden cocktail sticks (trimmed) or short lengths of wooden dowel
- Narrow black ribbon

Cut the paper or parchment into rectangular strips. On one side write 'This prisoner must die' or something similar. Wrap a length of double-sided Sellotape around the middle of two trimmed cocktail sticks. Lay the paper or parchment flat (writing side up) and carefully position a cocktail stick at each short end. Press the sellotaped stick down onto the paper and carefully begin to roll inwards. A piece of black ribbon sellotaped to one side can be used for fastening the scroll and hanging from the crown.

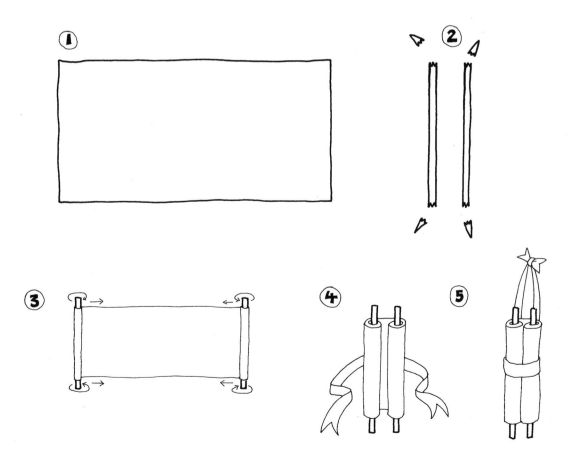

Question marks

These can be made from a variety of different materials including:

- Air hardening clay
- Plasticine
- Salt dough (see page 47)
- Pipe cleaners
- Card
- Wire coat hangers or wire from a DIY store
- Paint and varnish (optional)

If you choose to use air hardening clay or salt dough to create these shapes, remember to use a cocktail stick or something similar to pierce two holes (top and bottom) before baking or allowing to dry. (When dry and hard, these can be painted and/or varnished for a tough finish.) A small ball of clay or dough with a central hole can be suspended by gold thread to complete the question mark, which can then be hung by thread looped through the hole at the top.

Alternatively shape a length of wire and cover by wrapping in ribbon, strips of material, coloured paper, or papier-mâché (see page 47), which can then be painted. Whichever method you choose, don't forget to attach a loop of gold thread during the wrapping process for attaching to the crown.

The jewel of acceptance

Jesus is stripped and crowned

The Roman soldiers led Jesus away, and they began to taunt and mock him. They dressed him in a purple robe, and pressed a crown of thorns onto his head. Then they knelt before him and said, 'Hail, King of the Jews' and they beat him with a stick and spat on him. When they had had enough of teasing and abusing him, they stripped him of his purple robe and dressed him in his own clothes, before leading him away to be crucified.

Adapted from Mark 15:16-20

Reflection

Occasionally in the news we hear of someone who has been wrongly accused or imprisoned for a crime or wrongdoing they did not commit. In such unfortunate cases, there is often a public outcry with people demanding justice and campaigning to prove their innocence and clear their name. Nobody cried out to defend Jesus or to clear his name. Even Peter was too afraid to speak out on behalf of the Son of God. No one who had been cured by Jesus or experienced his holy power came forward to be a witness for his defence. Despite his innocence, Jesus did not try to defend himself. He did not argue or protest at the injustice of his trial. He calmly accepted the suffering and abuse he endured at the hands of the soldiers, because he understood that it was God's will and God's way. He accepted his suffering and the cross he was given to carry with dignity and courage. As Christians we need the jewel of acceptance if we are to allow God to work in and through our lives, and to fulfil his will despite the suffering and difficulties we will undoubtedly meet along the way.

Focus

- Can you recall any recent cases of injustice when people were wrongfully punished for a crime they did not commit?
- How do you imagine such an innocent person might have felt?
- How do you imagine their friends and family felt?
- Have you ever been accused of or blamed for something you didn't do?
- Read Matthew 26:67-68. Do you think Jesus found it easy to accept such mistreatment?
- As Christians today, what do you find difficult to accept in your life?

Prayer

Heavenly Father,
help us to accept your will
and follow your way.
At times of difficulty and doubt

give us the courage and faith
to remain true to you.
We make our prayer through Christ our King,
Amen.

Symbols

Lengths of purple cloth or paper and cut out garments are the symbols used to remind us of Christ's acceptance of his heavenly Father's will as he was taunted and abused.

Strips of cloth

You will need . . .

• Purple fabric or crepe paper

• *or* white paper and purple felt-tip pens or paint

• Scissors

Whether you choose to use material or paper, tear it into short lengths with frayed, irregular edges and weave them among the branches of Christ's crown.

Garments

You will need . . .

• Scraps of purple fabric or paper

• Thin card

• Gold thread

• Glue

• Scissors

• Felt-tip pens, crayons or paint (optional)

Cut out garment shapes from thin card. Cover these with fabric or purple paper glued into place, or simply colour and decorate the card with pens or similar. Use a loop of gold thread to attach the garments to the crown.

The jewel of strength (fortitude)

Jesus takes up his cross

The Roman soldiers led Jesus away and gave him a cross to carry to the place of execution at Golgotha, a name which means 'the place of the skull'.

Adapted from John 19:17

Reflection

By the time Jesus was finally given his cross to carry, he had already been spat on, beaten, crowned with thorns and cruelly abused by the soldiers and jeering crowds who looked on. Weakened by exhaustion and pain, the weight of the cross must have seemed almost unbearable. It took enormous strength to carry that cross, and to pick himself up and carry on even when he stumbled and fell. Such strength is not simply physical or muscular, it comes from deep inside a person, from their inner spirit itself. When someone has a problem or difficulty in their life, we sometimes refer to this as the 'cross they have to bear'. Such words remind us of the heavy cross Christ carried to Golgotha, together with the weight of the world's sins. Jesus understands our daily struggles and the temptation to simply give up when we feel that we can't carry on. With his help we can find the inner spiritual strength we need to allow us to carry the cross we have to bear in life instead of reluctantly dragging it.

Focus

- Does someone need to have a strong body to have a strong spirit?
- Read Luke 9:23-24. What kind of different 'crosses' do ordinary people have to bear?
- What cross or crosses do you personally carry in your own life? (Reflect silently and without sharing.)
- Do you ever ask Jesus to give you strength at times of difficulty?

Prayer

Heavenly Father,
send down your Spirit
and give us the strength
to overcome problems
and to pick ourselves up when we fall.
Help us to trust in your love above all else
and to carry our crosses cheerfully
as a sign of our love for you.
We make our prayer through Christ our King,
Amen.

Symbol

What better symbol than a cross to remind us of Christ's inner strength as he carried his own cross to Calvary.

Cross 1

You will need . . .

- Cocktail sticks (trimmed), twigs, lollipop sticks, pipe cleaners, cinnamon sticks or similar
- Wire bag closers or twine
- Scissors
- Gold thread (optional)

Cut two lengths of whichever material you choose to use for each cross. Make one piece shorter than the other to form the cross-piece. Bind these together with wire closers or lengths of twine. Either hang by thread from the crown or simply tuck the little crosses among its branches.

Cross 2

You will need . . .

- White card
- Scissors
- Paints, pens or crayons
- Gold thread (optional)

Cut small crosses from plain white card. Decorate and colour these according to choice and as before, either hang or tuck into the crown.

The jewel of humility

Simon helps Jesus

As they made their way to Golgotha (the place of the Skull), the soldiers forced a man called Simon, who came from Cyrene, to help Jesus to carry his cross.

Adapted from Matthew 27:32-33

Reflection

Simon walked behind Jesus and shared the weight of his cross. Perhaps the soldiers chose him from amongst the crowd because he looked strong and their struggling prisoner needed help if he was to complete his journey. We do not know whether Simon gave this assistance willingly or offered any words of comfort or encouragement to the condemned man whose burden he shared.

Sometimes we find it easier to offer rather than to accept help. Pride can make us believe that we can manage alone, and prevents us from asking for help when we need it. Usually it was Jesus who helped others, but he humbly accepted help when he needed it himself. We all need the help of one another, and it is not a sign of weakness or failure to reach out and ask for it.

Humility allows us to accept the goodness of others with appreciation and joy, and to share that goodness with others. Unless we are humble we cannot serve Christ and one another as he asks his followers to do.

Focus

- Imagine you are standing in the crowd. How do you feel when the soldiers choose you to help Jesus?
- What would you like to say to Jesus?
- How might Jesus react to your help?
- Have you ever been asked for help by someone? What happened?
- Have you ever had to ask for help yourself?
- Did you find it easy or difficult?
- How did it make you feel?
- In your opinion does humility show that a person is weak or strong?

Prayer

Heavenly Father,
help us to set our foolish pride aside.
Make us humble enough
to accept the help we ask for and receive,
and willing to offer it gladly to one another
with understanding and love.
We make our prayer through Christ our King,
Amen.

Symbol

A friendship bracelet and 'humility stone' are symbolic reminders of Christ's humility and readiness to accept a helping hand to carry his burden.

Friendship bracelet

You will need . . .

- A selection of coloured thread or wool
- Sellotape
- Scissors
- A piece of card
- A weight (a heavy book or similar)

Choose three different colours of thread or wool and cut equal lengths (these should be long enough to span a wrist). Knot the threads together at one end and tape to the piece of card. Place a weight on top of the card to hold it in position. Hold the central thread with one hand, and simply plait the other threads around it, just as you might plait hair. Complete the bracelet by firmly tying a knot at each end, and trim any excess thread or wool away. To make a wider bracelet, simply use more lengths of thread or thicker wool.

Humility stones

You will need . . .

- Smooth pebbles or stones
- Paints and paintbrushes
- Varnish (optional)
- Gold thread
- Fuse wire

Collect pebbles that are small and smooth, and carefully wash and dry them. Use the paint to decorate them with pictures or patterns. Allow the paint to dry thoroughly and then varnish them if you prefer a glossy finish.

We all have burdens or troubles that can weigh us down in life. As a sign of our willingness to share one another's troubles and to accept help when it is offered, exchange stones with someone else.

Carefully wind a piece of fuse wire around the pebble and form a small loop at the top. Attach a piece of gold thread to the wire and hang from the crown. (Alternatively, the stones could be placed at the foot of the cross.)

The jewel of compassion (being kind-hearted)

Jesus meets the women of Jerusalem

A great crowd of people followed Jesus, many of whom were women who wept sadly for him. Jesus said to them, 'Women of Jerusalem, do not be sad for me, but for yourselves and your children. A time will come when people will be glad that they have no children. They will say to the mountains, 'Fall on us!' and beg the hills to cover them. For if things such as these happen when the wood is green, what will happen when the wood is dry?'

Adapted from Luke 23:27-31

Reflection

Despite his own suffering, Jesus was moved by the sight of the women around him weeping. They cried at the pitiful sight of Jesus as he carried his cross to be crucified. He took time to stop and console them, trying to comfort them in their terrible sadness. He knew that his suffering would soon pass and after three days these women would be rejoicing instead. Their tears of sorrow would become tears of joy at the news of his resurrection. He didn't want them to pity and grieve for him, but instead to continue to have faith in him. At times of sadness in our own lives, Jesus is always there to offer us comfort and consolation. There were many occasions when his compassion for those who suffered moved him to cure the sick, feed the hungry, forgive sinners, and raise the dead to life. As his followers, he calls us to act with compassion and tenderness towards one another, and to trust in his love for us.

Focus

Can you recall any stories in which Jesus acted with compassion?

The following examples could be read within groups and acted out for everyone, or simply retold by the young people in their own words.

Read Matthew 9:27-29 (The cure of a blind man)
     Mark 6:35-44 (Miracle of loaves and fishes)
     Luke 7:36-50 (Jesus forgives a sinful woman)
     John 11:1-44 (Lazarus is raised to life)

- What do these stories tell us about Christian compassion? Has anyone ever comforted or consoled you?
- How did their kindness and compassion make you feel?
- In what ways can we act with compassion in our everyday lives?

Prayer

Heavenly Father,
you are compassion and love,
forgiving our mistakes, sharing our troubles,
and healing our sadness.

May we share Christ's living love
with our brothers and sisters
throughout the world.
We make our prayer through Christ our King,
Amen.

Symbol

Teardrops are the symbol of Christ's compassion for anyone who suffers or is sad.

Teardrops

You will need . . .

- Aluminium foil
- Scissors
- A thin knitting needle, kebab stick or similar
- Gold thread
- Sellotape

Cut long thin triangles from the foil (resembling the shape of an icicle) and an equal number of lengths of gold thread. Lie each foil triangle on its shiny side. Sellotape one end of your length of thread along the wide end of the foil (opposite the triangle's point) so that it projects from the foil at right angles. Now carefully wind the triangle of foil around a knitting needle or stick, beginning with the wide end which has the thread attached. Slowly slide the foil off the needle or stick and using your fingers, carefully form a teardrop shape. Tie several teardrops together and they are ready to hang.

(You could experiment with different materials and techniques to create teardrops, such as using blobs of clear varnish or glue and allowing them to dry on parchment paper. Remember to add threads or wire for the purposes of hanging, before they harden completely. Otherwise, craft and needle-work outlets offer a wide variety of teardrop shapes that are inexpensive and very effective.)

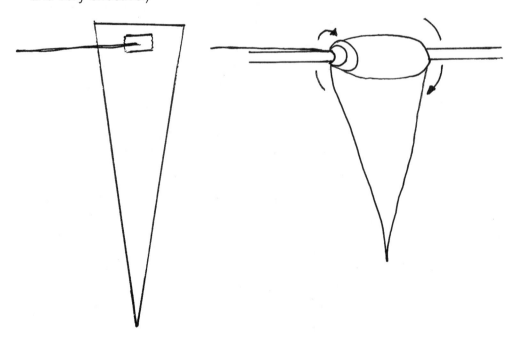

The jewel of forgiveness

Jesus is nailed to the cross

Two criminals were led out to be put to death with Jesus, and when they reached the place called the Skull, they were crucified, one on his right and the other on his left. Jesus prayed, 'Father, forgive them, for they do not understand what they are doing.'

While they threw dice to divide his clothes between them, some of the crowd jeered at him, 'If he is God's chosen one let him save himself; he's saved others!'

Even the soldiers mocked him as they came to offer him vinegar to drink, 'If you are King of the Jews, save yourself,' they called, and they hung a sign above him which read: 'This is the King of the Jews.'

Adapted from Luke 23:32-38

Reflection

Forgiveness is indeed wonderful. To forgive or to be forgiven restores peace and joy where there is conflict and unhappiness, and allows the process of healing to begin. Jesus personifies what forgiveness is; searching us for our innermost goodness and always ready to offer us another chance. It seems incredible to think that even as the soldiers nailed him to the cross, he had already forgiven them in his heart.

He had suffered being beaten and having thorns pressed onto his gentle head; insults, humiliation, taunting and jeering, and finally the pain of being nailed to the cross. Yet Christ forgave all of this, and acknowledged, 'They know not what they are doing.' God always seeks to forgive. He will find any possible reason, any reasonable excuse to understand and forgive us. All he searches for is sorrow in our hearts and the recognition of the wrong we have done. At times when we need to ask for God's forgiveness for ourselves, it helps to remember this scene as Jesus pleaded to his heavenly Father on our behalf. At times when we need to show forgiveness towards one another, his amazing example helps to inspire and encourage us. As Christians we are called to follow Christ's example of living love, forgiving one another as God forgives us.

Focus

Listen to or read the following parables.
What does each story tell us about forgiveness?

Matthew 18:21-35 (The unforgiving debtor)
Luke 7:36-50 (The sinful woman)
Luke 19:1-10 (The story of Zacchaeus)
Luke 15:12-32 (The prodigal son)

- Have you ever needed someone's forgiveness?

- Does being forgiven make us feel different? How?

- Is it easy to be a forgiving person? What gets in the way sometimes?

Story

Read the following story before allowing time for silent, personal reflection.

In the mid-1940s a gang smashed their way into a farmhouse in Germany and committed a crime that shocked the nation. In cold blood they machine-gunned the occupants – aged grandparents, four young children and the children's parents. Then they robbed the house and escaped. One of their victims, the father of the young family, though badly injured, managed to survive. Of the killers four were executed and four given life imprisonment. Eventually, one of them was due for parole but, having nowhere to go, he seemed destined to stay in prison until he died. But a local chemist, Wilhelm Hamelmann, asked the authorities if the prisoner could be released into his care. 'All men', he wrote by way of explanation, 'are my brothers.' Wilhelm Hamelmann was the man left for dead in the farmhouse twenty years earlier.

Prayer

Heavenly Father,
you forgive the unforgiven,
love the unloved,
and bring hope where there is despair.
May reconciliation and peace
change our hearts and lives
and help us to become more like you.
We make our prayer through Christ our King,
Amen.

Symbol

Even as he was being nailed to the cross and taunted by the crowd, Jesus forgave them. Nails and a placard are symbols for the jewel of forgiveness.

Nails 1

You will need . . .

- Nails
- Red paint or varnish (optional)
- Gold thread

Simply loop and tie some gold thread around the head of a nail, and hang from the crown. If appropriate, add a small amount of red paint or varnish to the tip to represent blood.

Nails 2

You will need . . .

- Cocktail sticks
- Grey poster paint
- Polystyrene tiles or pieces
- Gold thread

- Scissors
- Pencil with attached rubber, pen with barrel that unscrews or apple corer

Carefully remove the rubber from the top of a pencil to reveal the empty metal barrel. Use this to press down hard on a polystyrene tile to punch out small circular shapes. Alternatively, unscrew the barrel of a pen and use in a similar way. (An apple corer will produce a larger shape, which can always be trimmed to size.) Carefully trim one end of a cocktail stick to an appropriate length and add a blob of glue. Push this end into the polystyrene disc to form the head of the 'nail'. Allow to dry before painting grey and use gold thread to hang.

Nails 3

You will need . . .

- Pipe cleaners (black/brown/grey)
- Double-sided Sellotape
- Thin card
- Felt-tip pens
- Scissors
- Gold thread

Produce small circles of card by tracing around a suitable template or using a hole-punch, and colour these appropriately. Cut short lengths of pipe cleaners and bend one end at right angles. Attach a small piece of double-sided Sellotape to one side of the circle of the card and firmly press the bent pipe cleaner on. As before, use gold thread to hang.

Placard

You will need . . .

- Corrugated cardboard or plain card
- White paper or baking parchment
- Double-sided Sellotape or a glue stick
- Fine black pen
- Gold thread
- Pens or paints (optional)

For the placard cut a rectangle from the corrugated cardboard or card and colour appropriately. Cut a smaller identical shape from white paper or baking parchment. On one side write 'This is the King of the Jews' or something similar. (For larger quantities, you can simply photocopy a sheet with several templates on it.) Wrap the piece of paper around a pen or pencil (written side inwards) so that it curls slightly. Tape or glue the centre of the piece of paper onto the card, leaving the ends free. Attach a length of gold thread to the placard and hang from the crown.

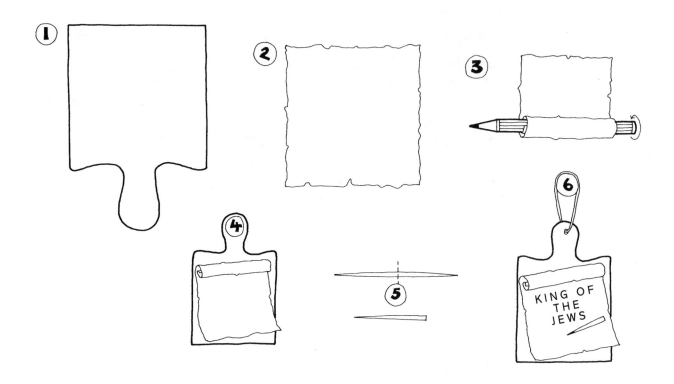

The jewel of hope

The good thief

One of the criminals hanging next to Jesus taunted him by saying, 'Aren't you the Christ? Can't you save yourself and us as well?'

But the other criminal scolded him, saying, 'Have you no fear of God? We deserve this punishment and are paying for our crimes, but this man has done nothing wrong!'

Then turning to Jesus he said, 'Jesus, when you come into your Kingdom remember me.'

Jesus answered him, 'This very day I promise that you will be with me in paradise.'

Adapted from Luke 23:39-43

Reflection

When earthquakes or floods strike parts of the world, the news is inevitably full of reports of tragedy and sadness. Our television screens reveal the terrible devastation and suffering such catastrophes bring, and the almost overwhelming sense of hopelessness. Scenes of people digging through rubble and ruins with their bare hands, reflect their hope that someone might still be alive having survived against all the odds. That hope keeps them going and sustains them through suffering, grief and difficulty.

For the thief sentenced to suffer on the cross next to Jesus, all hope seemed lost. Who would pity a common criminal, simply being punished for the wrong he had done? At such a time who would stand by him and offer him a ray of hope in the darkness of despair?

For the two thieves, their punishment reflected the seriousness of their offences, but how could the same be said of Jesus? He was 'guilty' of loving the world unconditionally in a way that had never been witnessed before, and that love would cost him his life.

The conversation between Jesus and the criminal who recognised his innocent goodness should fill all of us with enormous hope. When everything had seemed lost and completely hopeless, Jesus was able to promise the joy of paradise. Nothing is hopeless or impossible for God, and remembering this, we should never despair or completely give up hope. However far someone wanders from his love, whatever wrong they might commit, God does not abandon them. Sorrow can never come too late, wrongdoing can never be so terrible that God's forgiveness will be refused. By trusting and believing in Christ's unconditional love, the promise of sharing paradise with him is offered to us as well.

Focus

- Can you recall any stories in the news when a seemingly hopeless situation had a positive or happy outcome?
- Do you think that people are naturally hopeful or hopeless?

- Read John 14:1-4 and Romans 5:5-11. Why do these words encourage us to hope in Christ?
- What do you hope for your friends and family who have died?
- In today's world, how can we bring hope to the hungry, the sick and those who despair?

Prayer

Heavenly Father,
strengthen our faith in your love
and hope in your mercy.
Guide us along the paths
which lead us to you
so that we may share in the joy
and peace of paradise.
We make our prayer through Christ our King,
Amen.

Symbol

Jesus brings the light of hope in the darkness of despair. The symbol for hope is a moving picture scene.

Moving scene

You will need . . .

- Thin white card
- Scissors
- Felt-tip pens
- Gold thread
- Butterfly pins

Copy templates A and B onto thin white card, and cut out carefully. Colour one half of A black to represent darkness, and the other half yellow or similar to represent light. Colour template B as suggested. Carefully place template B on top of template A and use scissors to make a small hole in the centre. Insert a butterfly pin from front to back and open behind. Use the tab to change the background behind the cross. Attach a loop of thread to the top of the cross.

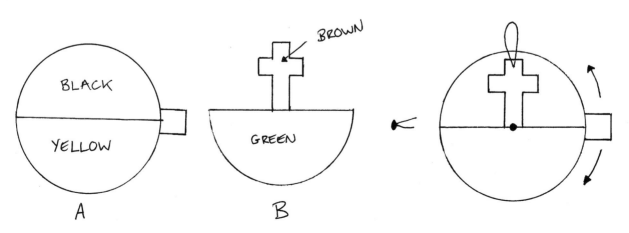

The jewel of thoughtfulness

Jesus and his mother

Mary the mother of Jesus and several other faithful women stood not far from his cross. With them was the disciple whom Jesus loved. Seeing them together, Jesus said to his mother, 'This is your son.' Then turning to the disciple he said, 'Here is your mother.' From that moment, Mary had a place in the disciple's home.

Adapted from John 19:25-27

Reflection

Imagine the scene: Jesus is hanging on the cross. His terrible suffering is almost over, and death is very close. Around him stand crowds of people who have gathered for the spectacle of execution. Yet in the midst of all this hustle and bustle, noise and pain, Jesus notices his mother and disciple standing near by.

Throughout Christ's short life, Mary his mother had experienced joy, wonder, disappointment and fear, and now she had to endure the greatest sadness of all, as she watched the son she loved dying on the cross. She had faithfully dedicated her life to loving and serving God, and to taking care of the Saviour he had entrusted to her care.

Christ's own suffering and pain are overshadowed by that of his grieving mother and friend. At that moment his thoughts are only for her and what will become of her. His thoughtfulness and concern for her well-being and future happiness prompt him to act to ensure that she will be lovingly cared for. At a time when it was natural to think only of his own suffering, he showed us how to think of others.

Being thoughtful takes effort. It means putting our selfishness aside and putting the needs of others before our own. Every thoughtful act, however large or small, however much it 'costs' us, is a precious jewel in Christ's crown.

Focus

- How would you describe or define a thoughtful person?
- What are their most important qualities?
- In your own life, who acts thoughtfully?
- How do you respond or act towards people who are thoughtful?
- Is the society and world in which we live a thoughtful place?
- What can we do to be more thoughtful and caring?
- Spend a few moments thinking about your day so far. Write down or discuss how you and those around you at home, at school or at work, have acted with thoughtfulness. (If appropriate, share thoughts and ideas.)

Prayer

Heavenly Father,
help us to be thoughtful people
who notice the needs of others
and respond with kindness and sensitivity.
May every thoughtful act
bring us closer to you.
We make our prayer through Christ our King,
Amen.

Symbol

The symbols to remind us of Christ's thoughtfulness towards his mother are a house and flowers.

Houses

Depending on the size you want, houses can be made in a variety of ways.

House 1

You will need . . .

- Cartridge paper or thin card
- Gold thread
- Sellotape and glue
- White or coloured paper
- Felt-tip pens
- Scissors

To make your own boxes trace the pattern on page 48 and make a card template. This can be scaled up or down to adjust the final size. Cut out the required number of 'houses' from coloured cartridge paper or thin card, and score carefully along the lines. Fold into shape and glue the tabs in place. Make a small hole in the 'roof' of the house and pass a loop of gold thread through. Cut out pieces of white or coloured paper for windows and doors, and use felt-tip pens to draw window frames, etc. Glue these onto the sides of the house. Houses of the time often had an outdoor staircase to the roof, so one of these can be added to the side of the box.

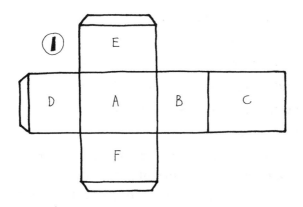

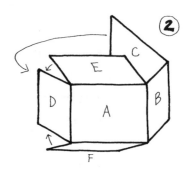

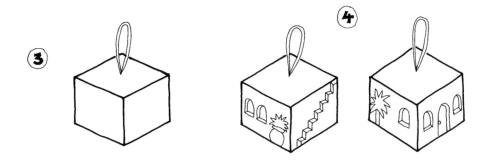

House 2

You will need . . .

- Empty matchboxes (small)
- Scissors
- Glue and Sellotape
- Coloured paper or material
- Gold thread
- Felt-tip pens or paint
- White paper

Glue or Sellotape three matchboxes together. Then cover with coloured paper, material or paint them. Draw and cut out windows and doors from white or coloured paper. Glue these onto the house and add any further decorative details you choose. Tape a loop of gold thread onto the roof of the house so that it is ready to hang.

House 3 (for larger houses)

You will need . . .

- Empty milk or juice cartons (washed and dried)
- Scissors
- Paint and paintbrushes
- Gold thread
- Paper and pens
- Glue

Decide how large you want your house to be and draw a line all the way around the carton. Carefully cut along this line with scissors, and then paint with bright, attractive colours. Allow to dry thoroughly before painting on windows and doors, or gluing on paper windows and door shapes you have cut out and coloured. Carefully make a hole in the roof 'ridge' with scissors and pass a loop of gold thread through if you choose to hang the house.

Flowers

These could be white roses to symbolise Mary, or blue flowers to represent 'Forget-me-nots'.

Flowers 1

You will need . . .

- Squares of white (or blue) tissue paper
- Sellotape
- Wire bag closers or fuse wire
- Gold thread (optional)

Take a square of tissue paper and turn it so that a corner is facing you. Then place another square on top at an angle to form the shape of an eight-pointed star. Holding the two pieces of tissue paper together, place your index finger in the middle and carefully scrunch the paper up and around it. Twist the paper in the middle into a stem that is held in place by a piece of Sellotape. Wind a bag closer or piece of fuse wire around the flower 'stem' to attach it to the crown, or group several flowers together in a posy and hang this using a loop of gold thread.

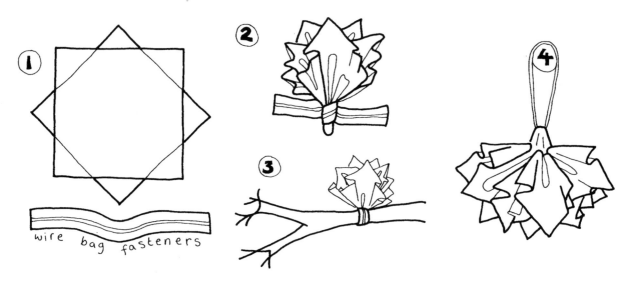

wire bag fasteners

Flowers 2

You will need . . .

- Scissors
- White card
- Sellotape
- Felt-tip pens or paint
- Pipe cleaners
- Glue

Cut out flower shapes from card and colour them on both sides. Make a small hole in the centre of each card flower (an adult should do this for younger children). Push a pipe cleaner through the hole and bend a short length over. Secure with a small piece of Sellotape. Dab a spot of glue in the centre of each flower over the pipe cleaner, and then disguise the pipe cleaner by sprinkling with glitter, covering with a piece of coloured card or fabric, or using buttons or sequins. When dry, the stem of the flower can be twined around the branches of the crown.

Flowers 3

You will need . . .

- Glue
- Florist's wire and green tape
- Scissors
- Tissue paper in a variety of colours

Layer three or four sheets of tissue paper together (these can be one or more colours). Cut out a flower shape and make a small hole in the centre. Make the centre of the flower by wrapping a small piece of tissue paper around one end of a piece of florist's wire, and taping it in place. Add the petals by threading the other end of the wire through the hole in the flower shape. Arrange the tissue petals carefully and secure in place with green tape, which can be wound around the wire to cover it and complete the flower.

You will need . . .

- Glue

The jewel of love

Jesus dies on the cross

About midday, darkness fell upon the land until three o'clock in the afternoon, and the curtain hanging in the Temple was torn in two. In a loud voice Jesus cried out 'Father, I place my spirit in your hands!' And then he died.

Adapted from Luke 23:44-46

Reflection

Jesus himself said, 'No one can have greater love than to lay down his life for his friends' (John 15:13). Christ's death on the cross is proof enough of God's love for us (John 3:16). We should be astonished that God became man, and then as that man died on the cross for us. He accepted death so that we might share in his risen life. Obedient to his heavenly Father's will, he accomplished the work he was given. He showed the height and depth of his love for his Father and for us. By his life and death, Jesus showed us what love really means. Unconditional love excludes no one, even those who choose to turn away and betray it. It is generous and forgiving, thoughtful and gentle. Such love can indeed be costly and carry a price, but Jesus expects no less from those who follow him: 'This is my commandment: love one another, as I have loved you' (John 15:12).

Focus

The word 'love' is commonly used to describe all manner of things. For example people might say that they 'love' a particular television programme or song.

- What does the word 'love' mean to you?
- In your own life, who loves you, and how do they express or show that love?
- How do you show others that you love them? Spend a few moments silently reflecting on how you might express your love for someone today. (It could be a school friend, parent, sister or brother perhaps.)
- Do you love everyone in the same way – at home, at school, in the world around you?
- Is it easy to love as Jesus loves?
- What challenges and difficulties do we experience and struggle with?

Prayer

Heavenly Father,
may the world recognise us
as your followers
by our love
for the sick, the homeless,
and the unwanted.

Help us to love one another
as we are loved by you.
We make our prayer through Christ our King,
Amen.

Symbol

The obvious symbol for the jewel of love is a heart. Several suggestions are given, but with a little imagination the ideas are endless.

Hearts 1

You will need . . .

- A sheet of thin paper or tracing paper
- Thin card
- Gold thread
- Scissors
- Glue
- Black pen
- Decorations, such as sequin waste, paper doyleys sprayed gold or silver, coloured tissue paper or cellophane.

Draw a heart shape and use to make a template from card. For each heart cut two such shapes from card and carefully remove the middle of both to leave a heart-shaped frame and 'window' in the middle. Place a piece of sequin waste, doyley, tissue paper or cellophane on top of one of the cut-out hearts, and with a pen carefully copy a heart shape which is slightly larger than the 'window' in the middle and cut this out. Spread glue on the inside of two card hearts and between them sandwich whichever decorative material you have chosen to use, together with a loop of gold thread at the top. Place a weight on top (a large book would do) and allow the heart to dry flat.

Hearts 2

You will need . . .

- Pieces of coloured card (various shapes)
- Paint
- Sponge
- Saucer
- Hole-punch
- Blue-tack or similar
- Gold thread
- Scissors
- Pencil

Fold a piece of card in half, and draw half a heart shape along the fold. Cut along the line you have drawn. You should now have a cut-out heart together with a piece of card with a heart-shaped window or space. These can be used as stencils to create heart shapes on the coloured pieces of card. Use a small piece of Blu-Tack to hold your stencil in position on the coloured card. Pour a little paint onto a saucer and dab this with a piece of sponge. Lightly dab the sponge on some scrap paper until you are confident to sponge over your stencils. Carefully lift the stencils off the card shapes, without smudging the paint. Allow to dry thoroughly before using a hole-punch to make a hole for a loop of gold thread. Your heart designs are now ready to hang.

Hearts 3

You will need . . .

- Red card or paper
- Gold thread
- Scissors
- Hole-punch
- Glue
- Decorative materials, such as glitter glue, sequins, foil shapes or paint

Cut heart shapes from folded red paper or card as described above (see *Hearts 2*). Decorate these with a variety of different materials, before making a hole with a hole-punch and hanging with gold thread.

Hearts 4

You will need . . .

- Scissors
- Glue or stapler
- Cotton wool or tissue paper
- Gold thread
- Felt squares or scraps of material
- Paper clips

Using a paper template, cut out heart shapes from the felt or fabric. Each heart will need two shapes with one slightly larger than the other. Place a little cotton wool or shredded tissue paper between the two pieces of fabric, and tuck a loop of gold thread in the top. Carefully glue or staple the two heart shapes together around the edge. If using glue, secure the edges with paper clips or similar until completely dry. (As an alternative filling you could use some scented lavender or pot potpourri.)

Hearts 5

You will need . . .

- Two heart-shaped biscuit cutters (one smaller than the other)
- Air hardening clay or salt dough
- Red paint or nail varnish
- Gold thread
- Cocktail stick

Roll out the clay or salt dough (see page 47) and cut out a heart shape using the larger cutter. Then take the smaller cutter and cut out a heart shape from the first heart. Carefully use a cocktail stick to make a hole in the top of each heart. Leave to dry in a warm airy place or harden in an oven. Decorate with red paint or nail varnish and allow to dry. Hang with a loop of gold thread.

The jewel of joy

The empty tomb

At sunrise on the Sunday morning, Mary of Magdala and another woman called Mary went to the tomb where Jesus was buried.

Suddenly the ground trembled violently like an earthquake, as an angel appeared, rolled the stone away from the tomb and sat on it. The angel dazzled like lightning, and the guards at the tomb were frozen with fear.

Then the angel spoke to the women saying, 'Do not be afraid! I know that you are looking for Jesus, who was crucified and buried here, but you will not find him because he is risen, just as he told you. Come and see for yourselves that he is gone! Now you must go to his disciples and tell them that he is risen, and you will see him again in Galilee. Go, and remember everything I have told you.'

Shaking with fear and excitement, the two women hurried from the tomb and ran to tell the disciples their marvellous news. On the way Jesus suddenly appeared and greeted them with the words, 'Peace be with you!' The women fell at his feet and worshipped the Lord. 'You have nothing to fear,' Jesus said. 'Tell my disciples to make their way to Galilee where they will see me for themselves.'

Adapted from Matthew 28:1-10

Reflection

When someone we know or love dies, we feel sad and alone. It hurts because we cannot see them any more or hear their voice, and we miss them. When Jesus died and was buried in the tomb, his disciples experienced all these feelings. Without Jesus, their world had fallen apart and seemed a much colder and darker place. They felt abandoned, alone and afraid of what the future held. Feelings such as these are shared by anyone who has experienced the grief of death. Christ's resurrection transforms this sadness to joy and brings hope instead of despair. We should not think of him as rising from the dead and then leaving us to cope alone. He remains with us, always present, unseen by our eyes and beyond our touch, but sharing all our troubles and pain. Through our faith we recognise more and more that he is present within and around us. Jesus said, 'I am the resurrection. Whoever believes in me, even though they die, they will live; anyone who lives and believes in me will never die' (John 11:25-26). By dying on the cross and rising from the dead, Jesus allows us to share his risen life when we die. Although parting from someone we love is painful and sad, we are comforted by the thought of their happiness and joy with Christ in his heavenly kingdom.

Focus

- Has someone close to you ever died?
- How did you feel?
- What do you believe happens when we die?

- Read John 14:1-3. Do these words of Jesus reassure you?
- What difference did Christ's resurrection make to his followers then and now?
- Depending on numbers, divide into two or more groups. Each group reads and reflects on either Matthew 27:45-50 or Matthew 28:5-8. On a large sheet of paper, write down words that might describe the feelings and mood of Christ's followers at that moment. Compare the lists for both passages and comment on the different language and expressions used.

Prayer

Heavenly Father,
transform our lives with your love
and fill them with the joy
of Christ's glorious resurrection
and the promise of eternal life.
We make our prayer through Christ our King,
Amen.

Symbol

The joy of Christ's resurrection from the dead is represented by Easter eggs, the traditional Easter symbol of new life. These can be presented in various ways.

Hanging eggs

You will need . . .

- Empty egg shells (washed and dried)
- Paints and paintbrushes
- Strips of coloured paper, thin ribbon, or gold thread
- Scissors
- Small plastic bottle
- Tissue paper
- Sellotape
- Cotton wool
- Glue, glitter, sequins (optional)
- Small fresh or paper flowers

Carefully paint the inside of an egg and allow to dry. Fill the plastic bottle with water. Place a piece of cotton wool over the lid and carefully rest the upside-down egg on top. Now carefully paint the outside of the egg and when dry, decorate with paints or add sequins or glitter. Once completely dry, gently tape lengths of coloured paper, ribbon or thread to the inside of the egg. Tuck some shredded tissue paper inside and complete with a small fresh or paper flower placed on top.

Paper eggs

You will need . . .

- White paper or card
- Scissors
- Gold thread
- Paint or felt-tip pens
- Decorative materials
- Glue
- Hole-punch

Cut out egg shapes from paper or card and decorate imaginatively. Make a hole at one end of each egg and hang with thread.

Papier-mâché eggs

You will need . . .

- Newspapers (Torn into small pieces or strips)
- Sellotape
- Gold thread
- Non-fungicidal wallpaper paste or flour and water paste
- Mixing bowl
- Paint
- Scissors
- Varnish (optional)
- Balloons

Partially inflate a balloon to the size of a small egg. Using either wallpaper or flour-and-water paste (see Recipes on page 47), dip small pieces of newspaper into the paste mixture and wrap them around the balloon. Change the direction you place the strips to give an even coverage. Use your fingers to smooth down the strips and wipe away any excess paste. Add a loop of gold thread as you work, and when you have achieved a satisfactory shape, allow the egg to dry in a warm place. (Remember to wash your hands!) When completely dry, paint and varnish for extra strength.

(Chicken wire or straight wire from gardening or DIY outlets can be bent and moulded to produce a basic egg shape which can then be covered with papier-mâché. Alternatively you could take papier-mâché moulds from large size eggs which have been blown (an adult should do this because of the salmonella risk). To do this, simply use a needle to pierce a hole in the top and bottom of an egg. Holding the egg over a cup or bowl, blow into the top hole and the egg's contents should emerge from the bottom hole.)

Alternatively you could dress the wooden cross that forms part of your display with paper flowers (as described on pages 38 and 39) to create a 'Resurrection Cross' which reflects the new life won for us by Christ's death and glorious resurrection from the dead.

Recipes

Handprint recipe

You will need . . .

- Wallpaper paste (fungicide free)
- Food colouring or powder paint
- Mixing bowl and spoon

Mix sufficient water with the wallpaper paste to achieve the consistency of thick cream. Add colour and mix well. Use this mixture to create hand- or footprints, but always remind children to take care and not to put the paint near their faces. A little paint can go a long way, so ensure that clothes are adequately protected (an old shirt with rolled-up sleeves is ideal), and you have access to washing facilities and towels.

Salt dough recipe

You will need . . .

- Two cups of plain flour
- One cup of salt
- One cup of water
- A mixing bowl

Mix the flour, salt and half of the water in a bowl. Add the remaining water gradually and knead to a firm dough. If the dough feels sticky, add more flour and knead again for 10 minutes. Leave to 'rest' for 30 minutes in an airtight container or plastic bag. To make your models last, bake them in an oven (250°F/120°C/Gas mark 1) until they are hard.

Papier-mâché recipe

You will need . . .

- Newspapers torn into small pieces or strips
- Non-fungicidal wallpaper paste or flour and water paste (see below)
- A mixing bowl

If you are using wallpaper paste, make it up according to the instructions on the packet. If you are using flour-and-water paste, add a small amount of cold water to approximately 50-80g of sieved plain white flour in a mixing bowl. Mix gently to make a paste, and add enough water to achieve the consistency of thin batter. Dip the small pieces of newspaper into the paste mixture and wrap them around your mould.

Change the direction you place the strips to give an even coverage. Use your fingers to smooth down the strips and wipe away any excess paste. Allow the mould to dry completely in a warm airy place. (Remember to wash your hands!) When completely dry, paint and varnish for extra strength.

Templates

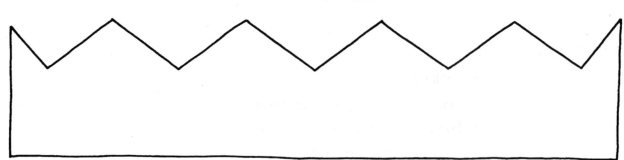

template for crown

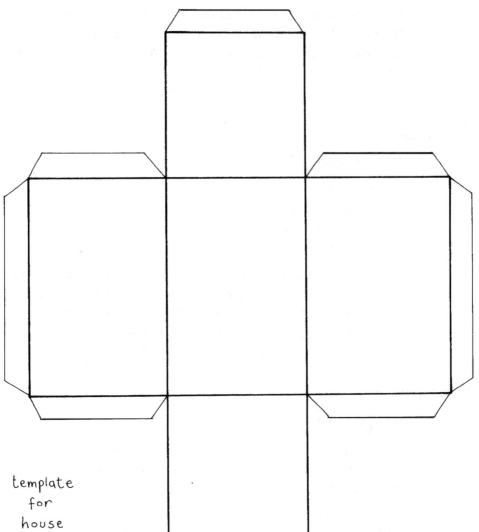

template
for
house